EFFECTIVE DIVERSITY RECRUITING STRATEGIES TO FUEL TALENT PIPELINE

Unlock the full potential of your organization by revolutionizing your approach to talent acquisition through powerful diversity recruiting strategies that fuel innovation, drive productivity, and maximize profitability.

FELIX TIH

TABLE OF CONTENTS

FORWARD

Diversity and inclusion are not just buzzwords but essential components of building a successful and sustainable organization. In today's globalized world, where the workforce is becoming increasingly diverse, it is crucial for companies to prioritize diversity recruiting to attract top talent from a wide range of backgrounds.

This book is a great resource for organizations that want to make their workplaces more diverse and open to everyone. The author has talked about everything important about diversity recruitment, from how to find and deal with unconscious bias to how to measure the success of diversity recruitment efforts.

As someone who has worked in many different organizations and fields, I have seen firsthand how a diverse workforce can be helpful. Not only does it bring fresh perspectives and innovative ideas to the table, but it also creates a sense of belonging and inclusivity among employees.

I think this book is a must-read for anyone who works on hiring, managing talent, or promoting diversity and inclusion. It gives a plan for making a workforce that is more diverse and welcoming, which can help organizations be more innovative, productive, and successful overall.

I commend the author for his thorough research, insightful analysis, and practical solutions. I am confident that this book will make a significant contribution to the ongoing conversation on diversity and inclusion in the workplace and will serve as a valuable resource for years to come.

Sincerely,

Maranga Sebastien Nguluwe

ACKNOWLEDGMENTS

We would like to express our gratitude to all those who have contributed to this book on diversity recruiting strategies.

First and foremost, we want to thank the individuals and organizations that have shared their insights and experiences with us. Without your contributions, this book would not have been possible.

We would also like to thank our team of editors, designers, and project managers, who worked tirelessly to bring this book to life. Your dedication and hard work have been invaluable.

We want to thank our families and friends for all the support and encouragement they gave us while we were writing.

Finally, we want to express our deepest gratitude to the readers of this book. We hope that the strategies and best practices outlined in these pages will inspire you to create a more diverse and inclusive workforce.

Thank you all for your support and collaboration.

WHO THIS BOOK (AND MESSAGE) IS FOR?

This book is valuable for those interested in understanding the importance of diversity and inclusion in the workplace and how they can benefit organizations in terms of innovation, productivity, and profitability. This book is important for:

1. HR professionals and recruiters who want to expand their knowledge and skills in diversity recruiting to attract and retain top talent from diverse backgrounds.

2. Business leaders and managers who recognize the importance of building a diverse workforce to drive innovation and growth and want to learn how to implement effective diversity recruitment strategies.

3. This book is crucial for startups, as they face a unique set of challenges when it comes to diversity and inclusion. Startups are often founded by small groups of people with similar backgrounds and experiences, which can lead to a lack of diversity in their initial team. This homogeneity can hinder their ability to understand and appeal to a broad range of customers and limit their potential for growth and innovation. Moreover, startups often have limited resources and time, which can make it challenging to prioritize diversity and inclusion efforts. This book provides startups with practical strategies and actionable advice to help them attract and retain diverse talent, foster a culture of inclusion, and drive innovation and growth. By implementing the principles outlined in this book, startups can gain a competitive edge and position themselves for long-term success.

4. Diversity and inclusion advocates who are passionate about creating a more inclusive workplace and want to understand the best practices for attracting and retaining diverse talent.

5. Job seekers who are interested in understanding how organizations approach diversity and inclusion in their recruitment efforts and want to prepare themselves for the job search process.

6. Students and academics who are studying diversity and inclusion in the workplace and want to gain a practical understanding of how organizations can effectively recruit and retain diverse talent.

INTRODUCTION

The benefits of diversity and inclusion in the workplace are well documented. Research shows that diverse teams are more innovative, productive, and profitable. However, building a diverse workforce requires a deliberate effort, especially in the recruitment process.

While diversity recruiting strategies are an essential component of creating a diverse workforce, they are only part of the equation. An organization's culture plays a critical role in attracting and retaining diverse talent. Without an inclusive culture, diverse employees may feel isolated, undervalued, or unsupported, leading to higher turnover rates and reduced productivity.

An inclusive culture is one where all employees feel safe expressing their opinions, ideas, and perspectives without fear of judgment or discrimination. It is a culture that values diversity and encourages collaboration, respect, and open communication. Creating such a culture takes time and effort, but the benefits are worth it. Not only does an inclusive culture help attract and retain diverse talent, but it also fosters creativity, innovation, and better decision-making.

In this book, we'll look at effective ways to hire people from different backgrounds to fill the talent pipeline.

CHAPTER 1 : UNDERSTANDING DIVERSITY

Recruiting a diverse workforce is critical for an organization's success in today's global economy. Diverse teams bring new perspectives, ideas, and experiences, which can lead to increased innovation, creativity, and productivity. However, diversity recruiting requires a deep understanding of what diversity means and how it can be defined in the workplace. In this chapter, we will explore the concept of diversity and its importance in the recruitment process.

Diversity is the range of differences between people, such as their race, ethnicity, gender, age, religion, sexual orientation, socioeconomic status, physical abilities, and cultural background, among other things. It's important to remember that diversity isn't just about race or gender or other things that can be seen. It also encompasses differences in thoughts, ideas, and experiences that come from a variety of backgrounds.

I.   Why Diversity Matters

Diversity in the workplace is crucial for several reasons. First, it promotes innovation and creativity. When people from different backgrounds come together, they bring unique perspectives and ideas, which can lead to more innovative solutions to business problems. Second, diversity can enhance productivity. Diverse teams tend to be more collaborative and better at problem-solving, leading to better business outcomes. Finally, diversity promotes inclusivity and can help build a strong company culture that values all employees and their contributions.

II. Benefits of Diversity Recruiting

Diversity recruiting offers several benefits to organizations. First, it can improve a company's reputation and brand. Organizations that prioritize diversity and inclusion are more likely to attract and retain top talent. Second, diversity recruiting can enhance the company's overall performance. Diverse teams are more likely to produce better business outcomes and higher levels of innovation. Finally, diversity recruiting can create a culture of inclusivity, which can lead to higher employee engagement, job satisfaction, and retention rates.

III. Key Challenges in Diversity Recruiting

Despite the benefits of diversity recruiting, there are several challenges that organizations may face. One of the main challenges is bias, both conscious and unconscious. Recruiters may have personal biases that influence their decision-making, leading to less diverse hiring outcomes. Another challenge is the lack of diversity in the candidate pool. This can be a result of a lack of outreach to diverse communities or a lack of diversity in the industry itself. Finally, legal, and regulatory requirements can also pose a challenge, as organizations must ensure compliance with anti-discrimination laws.

IV. Best Practices in Diversity Recruiting

To overcome these challenges and promote diversity recruiting, organizations should adopt several best practices. These include:

- **Define diversity:** Organizations should define what diversity means to them and how it aligns with their values and goals. This can help recruiters figure out what they're looking for in a diverse candidate and make sure they're taking all aspects of diversity into account.

- **Develop a diversity recruitment plan:** Organizations should develop a comprehensive diversity recruitment plan that includes outreach to diverse communities, job postings in diverse publications, and partnerships with diversity-focused organizations.

- **Train recruiters on unconscious bias:** Organizations should teach recruiters about unconscious bias and how it can affect the hiring process. This can help recruiters recognize their biases and make more objective hiring decisions.

- **Diversify the candidate pool:** Organizations should take proactive steps to diversify the candidate pool. This can include expanding outreach efforts, using blind resume screening, and partnering with diversity-focused recruitment firms.

- **Foster an inclusive culture:** Organizations should create an inclusive culture that values diversity and promotes open communication and collaboration. This can help attract and retain diverse talent and create a positive work environment for all employees.

Diversity recruiting is critical for organizations looking to stay competitive in today's global economy. By understanding the importance of diversity and defining it in the workplace, organizations can develop effective diversity recruiting strategies that enhance their overall performance and create a culture of inclusivity. By adopting best practices such as developing a diversity recruitment plan, training recruiters on unconscious bias, and fostering an inclusive culture, organizations can overcome the challenges of diversity recruiting and attract a diverse pool of talented candidates.

It's also important to realize that recruiting for diversity is an ongoing process that needs to be evaluated and improved all the time. Organizations should regularly assess their diversity recruitment efforts and adjust as needed to ensure they are meeting their goals and creating a diverse and inclusive workplace.

In the next chapter, we explored how organizations can create a culture of diversity and inclusion that supports diversity recruiting efforts and fosters a positive work environment for all employees. We discussed the key elements of an inclusive culture, including leadership commitment, employee engagement, and diversity and inclusion training. We also provided practical tips for creating an inclusive culture and sustaining diversity recruiting efforts over time.

CHAPTER II: CRAFTING INCLUSIVE JOB DESCRIPTIONS

Job descriptions serve as the initial point of contact between job seekers and organizations. It is crucial that job descriptions be crafted to attract a diverse pool of applicants. The language used in job descriptions can have a significant impact on the diversity of applicants. Words and phrases that imply bias or exclusion can discourage qualified candidates from applying. Organizations should aim to create job descriptions that promote diversity and inclusivity. In this chapter, we will explore the importance of crafting inclusive job descriptions and provide practical tips for doing so.

I.   Why Inclusive Job Descriptions Matter

Inclusive job descriptions matter for several reasons. Firstly, they can help attract a diverse pool of applicants. When job descriptions use inclusive language, they send a signal that the organization values diversity and is committed to creating an inclusive workplace. This, in turn, can attract candidates from a variety of backgrounds. Secondly, inclusive job descriptions can help reduce unconscious bias. Research has shown that job descriptions that use gender-neutral language can help reduce gender bias in the hiring process. Finally, inclusive job descriptions can help create a more diverse and inclusive workplace. By attracting a diverse pool of applicants, organizations can increase their chances of hiring a diverse workforce.

II.   How to Craft Inclusive Job Descriptions

Crafting inclusive job descriptions requires attention to language and a commitment to diversity and inclusivity. The following are some practical tips for creating job descriptions that promote diversity and inclusivity.

- **Avoid gendered language:** Job descriptions should use gender-neutral language to avoid excluding candidates based on their gender. For example, instead of using "he" or "she," use "they" or "the successful candidate."

- **Use inclusive language:** Job descriptions should use inclusive language that welcomes applicants from all backgrounds. Avoid using language that could be perceived as discriminatory. For example, instead of using "young and energetic," use "enthusiastic and dynamic."

- **Avoid jargon:** Job descriptions should be written in plain language to ensure that they are easily understood by all candidates. Avoid using jargon or technical terms that may be unfamiliar to some applicants.

- **Highlight diversity and inclusion:** Job descriptions should show how committed the company is to diversity and inclusion. This can be done by including a statement on diversity and inclusion in the job description.

- **Be specific:** Job descriptions should be specific about the job's requirements and qualifications. This can help attract qualified candidates from a variety of backgrounds.

- **Consider accessibility:** Job descriptions should be accessible to candidates with disabilities. This can be done by ensuring that the job description is available in accessible formats such as HTML or PDF.

III.   Examples of Inclusive Language:

The following are examples of inclusive language that can be used in job descriptions:
"We welcome applicants from all backgrounds"
"The successful candidate will have experience working with diverse teams"
"We are committed to creating an inclusive workplace"
"We encourage applicants with disabilities to apply"
"We value diversity and inclusivity in our workplace"

IV.   Examples of Language to Avoid:

The following are examples of language that can be perceived as discriminatory and should be avoided:

"We are looking for a young and energetic candidate"

"The successful candidate must be physically fit"
"We are seeking a candidate with excellent English language skills"
"We need a candidate who is a good cultural fit"
"We are looking for someone with a traditional background"

Inclusive job descriptions are a crucial component of diversity recruiting strategies. They can help attract a diverse pool of applicants, reduce unconscious bias, and create a more diverse and inclusive workplace. Organizations should aim to use inclusive language in their job descriptions and avoid language that could be perceived as discriminatory. By crafting inclusive job descriptions, organizations can increase their chances of hiring a diverse workforce and creating a workplace where all employees feel valued and included.

V. Tips for Ensuring Inclusive Language in Job Descriptions

- **Use tools to check for bias:** Several tools are available to help check job descriptions for bias. These tools use artificial intelligence to identify language that may be biased or exclusionary. Examples of such tools include Textio, Gender Decoder, and Joblint.

- **Conduct a diversity audit:** Organizations can conduct a diversity audit of their job descriptions to figure out what needs to be changed. This can be done by reviewing job descriptions for language that may be biased or exclusionary and making changes accordingly.

- **Seek input from diverse employees:** Employees from different backgrounds can provide valuable insights into how job descriptions can be made more inclusive. Organizations can seek input from diverse employees on how to make job descriptions more welcoming to candidates from all walks of life.

- **Regularly review and update job descriptions:** Job descriptions should be reviewed and updated regularly to ensure that they continue to be inclusive. As organizations evolve and change, so should their job descriptions. Regularly reviewing and updating job descriptions can help ensure that they remain inclusive and relevant.

Crafting inclusive job descriptions is an essential step in building a diverse and inclusive workforce. Using inclusive language in job descriptions can help attract a diverse pool of candidates and reduce unconscious bias in the hiring process. Organizations should aim to use gender-neutral language, avoid jargon, highlight diversity and inclusivity, and be specific about job requirements and qualifications.

Additionally, organizations should regularly review and update job descriptions to ensure that they remain inclusive and relevant. By crafting inclusive job descriptions, organizations can increase their chances of hiring a diverse workforce and creating a workplace where all employees feel valued and included.

CHAPTER 3: BUILDING RELATIONSHIPS WITH DIVERSITY-FOCUSED ORGANIZATIONS

Building a diverse workforce is crucial for the success of any organization. One effective way to achieve this is by partnering with organizations that focus on diversity. These organizations are committed to promoting diversity and inclusion in the workplace and can help organizations reach a diverse pool of candidates. In this chapter, we will discuss how to identify and build relationships with diversity-focused organizations.

I.   Identifying Diversity-Focused Organizations:

The first step in building relationships with diversity-focused organizations is to identify them. Some organizations focus on specific demographics, such as women, people of color, or individuals with disabilities. Other organizations focus on promoting diversity and inclusion in general.

II. **Below are some examples of diversity-focused organizations**

- **National Black MBA Association:** This organization focuses on promoting the educational and professional development of African American professionals.

- **Society for Women Engineers:** This organization is dedicated to promoting women in engineering and technology.

- **Disability:IN:** This organization is committed to promoting the inclusion of individuals with disabilities in the workplace.

- **National Society of Hispanic MBAs:** This organization focuses on promoting the educational and professional development of Hispanic professionals.

- **Out & Equal Workplace Advocates:** This organization is dedicated to promoting workplace equality for the LGBTQ+ community.

III. **Approaching Diversity-Focused Organizations**

Once you have identified diversity-focused organizations, the next step is to approach them for partnership opportunities. Here are some tips for approaching these organizations:

- **Do your homework:** Before reaching out to an organization, research their mission and values to ensure that they align with your organization's goals. This will also help you tailor your approach to their specific focus.

- **Attend events:** Attend events hosted by diversity-focused organizations to meet their members and learn more about their work.

- **Be clear about your goals:** Clearly communicate your organization's commitment to diversity and your specific goals for partnering with the organization.

- **Offer value:** Offer something of value to the organization, such as sponsorship or volunteering opportunities.

- **Follow up:** After reaching out to an organization, follow up with them to ensure that they received your message and to discuss next steps.

IV. Building Relationships with Diversity-Focused Organizations:

Building relationships with diversity-focused organizations takes time and effort. However, these relationships can lead to a diverse pool of candidates and a more inclusive workplace culture. Here are some tips for building strong relationships with diversity-focused organizations:

- **Engage in ongoing communication:** Maintain open communication with the organization to discuss upcoming events and opportunities for collaboration.

- **Attend events:** Attend events hosted by the organization to show your support and engage with their members.

- **Provide support:** Offer support to the organization, such as by sponsoring an event or providing volunteer opportunities for your employees.

- **Be consistent:** Demonstrate your commitment to diversity and inclusion in all aspects of your organization.

- **Celebrate wins:** Celebrate wins with the organization, like the hiring of a person from a different background, to strengthen your relationship and show your support.

Partnering with diversity-focused organizations is an effective way to reach a diverse pool of candidates and promote a more inclusive workplace culture. Identifying the right organizations and approaching them with a clear goal and value proposition can lead to successful partnerships. Building strong relationships with these organizations requires ongoing communication, a consistent commitment to diversity and inclusion, and celebrating successes together. By building relationships with diversity-focused organizations, organizations can create a more diverse and inclusive workforce and achieve their business goals.

V.   Examples of Successful Partnerships:

Here are some examples of successful partnerships between organizations and diversity-focused groups:

- **PwC and Disability:IN:** PwC has partnered with Disability:IN to promote the inclusion of individuals with disabilities in the workplace. Through this partnership, PwC has committed to hiring individuals with disabilities and providing accommodations for their needs.

- **IBM and the National Society of Black Engineers:** IBM has partnered with the National Society of Black Engineers to promote the professional development of African American engineers. This partnership includes mentoring programs, scholarships, and networking opportunities.

- **Accenture and Out& Equal Workplace Advocates:** Accenture has partnered with Out & Equal Workplace Advocates to promote workplace equality for the LGBTQ+ community. This partnership includes sponsoring events, providing volunteer opportunities for employees, and promoting diversity and inclusion in the workplace.

- **Walmart and the National Society of Hispanic MBAs:** Walmart has partnered with the National Society of Hispanic MBAs to promote the professional development of Hispanic professionals. This partnership includes scholarships, mentorship programs, and leadership development opportunities.

- **Microsoft and the Society for Women Engineers:** Microsoft has partnered with the Society for Women Engineers to promote the professional development of women in engineering and technology. This partnership includes mentorship programs, scholarships, and support for women-owned businesses.

Partnering with diversity-focused organizations can be an effective way to promote diversity and inclusion in the workplace. Organizations can create a more diverse and inclusive workforce by finding the right organizations, approaching them with a clear goal and value proposition, and building strong relationships. Successful partnerships with organizations that care about diversity can lead to a more diverse pool of candidates, more engaged employees, and more creativity and productivity.

CHAPTER 4: DIVERSIFYING SOURCING CHANNELS

Diversity and inclusion have become critical aspects of modern recruitment strategies. Organizations that embrace diversity are more likely to attract and retain top talent, increase innovation and productivity, and build strong relationships with customers and stakeholders. However, recruiting a diverse workforce requires expanding sourcing channels beyond traditional recruitment methods. In this chapter, we will explore how organizations can diversify their sourcing channels to attract a more diverse pool of candidates.

I.   Leveraging Social Media

Social media platforms have become an integral part of modern recruitment strategies. They provide a cost-effective way to reach a large audience and promote open positions.

Social media has become an essential tool for recruiting diverse candidates.

According to a survey by Jobvite, 73% of recruiters have successfully hired a candidate through social media. LinkedIn, Facebook, and Twitter are the most used social media platforms for recruiting purposes.

LinkedIn is the best social media site for professional networking, which makes it a great place to find candidates from different backgrounds. Organizations can use LinkedIn to post job listings, search for candidates, and reach out to potential candidates directly. LinkedIn also has groups and forums for specific demographics or industries, which makes it easier to connect with potential candidates from groups that don't get as much attention.

Facebook is the most popular social media platform worldwide, with over 2.8 billion monthly active users. It can be an effective tool for targeting diverse candidates. Facebook allows organizations to create job listings and target them at specific demographics or locations. For example, an organization looking to recruit diverse candidates can target job ads to users who identify as members of underrepresented groups or live-in communities with diverse populations.

You can use **Twitter** to find people to hire by posting job ads or contacting potential candidates directly. **Hashtags** can also be used to reach a wider audience. For example, using **hashtags** like **#diversityinclusion** or **#diversityrecruitment** can help organizations reach a more diverse audience.

However, to attract a diverse pool of candidates, it is essential to leverage social media in the right way. Here are some tips for leveraging social media to attract diverse candidates:

Use inclusive language: Use inclusive language that welcomes candidates from all backgrounds. Avoid words and phrases that imply bias or exclusion.

Share diverse stories: Share stories of successful employees from diverse backgrounds. This can help showcase the organization's commitment to diversity and inclusion.

Target diverse audiences: Use social media platforms that are popular among diverse audiences. For example, LinkedIn and Twitter are popular among professionals, while Instagram and Snapchat are popular among younger demographics.

Use visuals: Use visuals such as photos and videos that showcase the organization's diverse workforce. This can help potential candidates see themselves as part of the organization.

Engage with diverse communities on social media. Join groups and participate in discussions to build relationships with potential candidates.

II.   Niche Job Boards

Niche job boards are job search websites that focus on specific industries or demographics.

Niche job boards cater to specific industries, professions, or demographics. They can be a valuable source of diverse candidates. For example, organizations can use job boards like Tech Ladies or Hire Autism to target underrepresented groups in the technology or disability communities.

There are also job boards that focus specifically on diversity and inclusion. These job boards are designed to connect organizations with diverse candidates. Examples of diversity job boards include DiversityJobs.com, iHispano, and BlackJobs.com.

They can be an effective way to reach a more diverse pool of candidates. Here are some tips for leveraging niche job boards to attract diverse candidates:

Identify relevant job boards: Identify job boards that focus on specific industries or demographics. For example, Women in Technology International is a job board that focuses on promoting women in the technology industry.

Use inclusive language: Use inclusive language in job postings on niche job boards. This can help attract a more diverse pool of candidates.

Participate in events: Participate in events hosted by niche job boards. This can help build relationships with potential candidates.

Leverage referrals: Leverage referrals from existing employees or industry contacts to attract candidates from diverse backgrounds.

III.   Other Non-Traditional Sourcing Channels

Expanding sourcing channels beyond traditional recruitment methods can help organizations attract a more diverse pool of candidates. Here are some non-traditional sourcing channels that organizations can leverage:

Referral programs: Referral programs can help organizations attract candidates from diverse backgrounds. However, it is essential to ensure that the referral program is inclusive and rewards employees for referring candidates from diverse backgrounds.

Alumni networks: Alumni networks can be an effective way to reach a more diverse pool of candidates. Organizations can partner with universities and colleges to promote job opportunities to alumni.

Industry events: Industry events can be an effective way to build relationships with potential candidates from diverse backgrounds. Organizations can participate in conferences and events to network and promote job opportunities.

IV.   Measuring Success

Measuring the success of sourcing channels is essential to optimizing recruitment strategies. Metrics like the number of applications, interviews, and hires can be used to track the effectiveness of sourcing channels. However, to measure the success of diversity recruitment strategies, organizations must also track diversity metrics.

Diversity metrics include the number and percentage of diverse candidates who apply, are interviewed, and ultimately are hired. These metrics can help organizations identify gaps in their recruitment process and adjust their strategies accordingly.

It is also important to measure the impact of specific sourcing channels on diversity metrics. For example, an organization can track the percentage of diverse candidates who applied through job boards, social media, or employee referrals. This data can be used to adjust recruitment strategies to better reach underrepresented groups.

Measuring the success of sourcing strategies is essential to optimizing recruitment efforts continually. Here are some metrics that organizations can use to measure the success of their sourcing strategies:

Diversity of applicant pool: Keep track of the diversity of the applicant pool to make sure that sourcing strategies are bringing in a diverse group of candidates.

Time-to-hire: Keep track of how long it takes to hire candidates from different backgrounds to make sure that sourcing strategies aren't slowing down the hiring process.

V.   Employee Referral Programs

Employee referral programs can be a powerful tool for sourcing diverse candidates. However, they can also perpetuate a lack of diversity within an organization if not managed properly. To ensure a diverse candidate pool, organizations can incentivize employees to refer diverse candidates. For example, an organization can offer a higher referral bonus for diverse candidates or host events specifically for diverse employees to network and refer potential candidates.

Track the participation rate of employees in the referral program to ensure that the program is inclusive and effective.

Expanding sourcing channels beyond traditional recruitment methods can help organizations attract a more diverse pool of candidates with a variety of experiences, backgrounds, and perspectives. This can lead to a stronger and more innovative team, as diverse viewpoints can bring fresh ideas and approaches to problem-solving. Additionally, having a diverse workforce can help organizations better understand and serve a diverse customer base, leading to increased customer loyalty and revenue. Overall, diversifying sourcing channels is an important step in building a more inclusive and successful organization.

Expanding sourcing channels is essential to building a diverse talent pipeline. Traditional recruitment methods may not be effective in reaching underrepresented groups. Organizations can leverage social media, niche job boards, and employee referral programs to reach a more diverse candidate pool. Measuring the success of sourcing strategies is essential to optimizing recruitment strategies and building a diverse workforce.

CHAPTER 5: USING BLIND HIRING TECHNIQUES

Unconscious bias can often show up during the hiring process and cause qualified candidates to be turned away because of their gender, race, age, or other personal traits. Blind hiring is a technique used to mitigate the effects of unconscious bias by removing personal identifying information from job applications, thus enabling recruiters to focus solely on a candidate's skills and qualifications. In this chapter, we will explore the benefits of blind hiring and discuss how to implement this technique in the recruitment process. We will provide examples of successful blind hiring programs and explain how to measure their effectiveness.

I.   What is Blind Hiring

Blind hiring is a recruitment strategy that involves removing personal identifying information from a job application. The aim of this technique is to reduce the impact of unconscious bias on the recruitment process.

Recruiters focus solely on the candidate's qualifications, skills, and experience, without being influenced by any demographic information.

Blind hiring is not a new concept; it has been used by organizations for many years to promote diversity and inclusion. In recent years, it has gained popularity due to the growing awareness of unconscious bias and the need for more diverse and inclusive workplaces.

II.   Types of Blind Hiring

There are different types of blind hiring techniques, each with its own benefits and challenges. Some of the most common types of blind hiring include:

- **Name-Blind Hiring:** This involves removing the candidate's name from their application, resume, or cover letter. This technique aims to eliminate unconscious bias based on the candidate's name, which may be associated with a particular gender, race, or ethnicity.

- **Skill-Based Hiring:** This technique focuses on a candidate's skills and abilities rather than their work experience or education. This is achieved by asking candidates to complete a skills-based test or project, which is then evaluated anonymously.

- **Education-Blind Hiring:** This technique involves removing the candidate's educational background from their application. This is done to reduce the impact of unconscious bias based on the prestige of the institution or degree.

- **Interview-Blind Hiring:** This technique involves conducting interviews without seeing the candidate. This can be achieved through audio or video interviews or by using blind hiring software that disguises the candidate's voice or appearance.

III.   Benefits of Blind Hiring

Blind hiring, which is a recruitment technique that involves removing identifying information from resumes and applications, can offer several benefits to organizations, including:

- **Reducing Unconscious Bias:** Blind hiring removes personal information that can lead to unconscious bias in the recruitment process. This helps to ensure that candidates are evaluated solely on their qualifications and skills rather than their demographics.

- **Increasing Diversity:** Blind hiring can help increase diversity in the workplace. By removing identifying information, recruiters are more likely to evaluate candidates based on their skills and qualifications, which can lead to a more diverse pool of candidates.

- **Improving Candidate Experience:** Blind hiring can also improve the candidate experience. Candidates may feel more confident that they will be evaluated fairly and objectively, leading to a positive impression of the organization.

- **Enhancing Brand Reputation:** Organizations that implement blind hiring techniques can enhance their brand reputation as diversity and inclusion leaders. This can help to attract top talent and improve customer loyalty.

IV.   Challenges of Blind Hiring

Despite the benefits of blind hiring, there are also several challenges that organizations may face when implementing this technique. Some of the common challenges include:

- **Difficulty in Implementing:** Blind hiring requires significant effort to implement effectively. This may include changes to recruitment processes, technology, and training.

- **Limited Information:** Blind hiring can lead to limited information about a candidate's background, which may be important for certain roles or industries.

- **Possibility of Reverse Discrimination:** Blind hiring can also lead to the possibility of reverse discrimination, in which candidates are chosen based on their demographics rather than their qualifications.

- **Difficulty in Measuring Effectiveness:** It can be hard to measure how well blind hiring works because it removes identifying information from applications, which makes it hard to track diversity metrics. Also, blind hiring may not get rid of bias because unconscious bias can still show up in other ways, like the way people use language and the job requirements. So, organizations should also think about other ways to recruit people from diverse backgrounds to go along with blind hiring and make sure they have a full approach to diversity and inclusion.

Utilizing skills-based assessments is another approach to put blind hiring practices into practice. Skills-based exams can assist hiring managers in evaluating candidates based on their skills and qualifications rather than only looking at resumes and cover letters. Unconscious prejudices based on things like school background or professional experience can be eliminated with this technique.

One popular skill-based assessment is a coding challenge, which is commonly used in the tech industry. Candidates are given a coding problem and asked to provide a solution. This assessment helps evaluate the candidate's coding skills without bias towards factors such as education or work experience.

Another example of a skills-based assessment is a work sample test. This type of assessment asks candidates to complete a project that is related to the job they are applying for. For example, a graphic design candidate might be asked to create a logo for a fictitious company. This type of assessment can help hiring managers evaluate the candidate's skills and creativity without relying solely on their resume and cover letter.

It is important to note that blind hiring techniques should not be used in isolation. Even though they can help get rid of unconscious bias, they should be used with other diversity hiring strategies to make sure that the pool of candidates is as diverse as possible. Additionally, blind hiring techniques may not be suitable for all types of roles. For example, blind hiring may not be practical for roles that require face-to-face interaction with customers or clients.

Measuring the effectiveness of blind hiring techniques can be challenging. It is important to establish metrics before implementing blind hiring techniques to ensure that progress can be tracked. Metrics such as the percentage of diverse candidates in the applicant pool, the percentage of diverse candidates who make it to the interview stage, and the percentage of diverse candidates who are ultimately hired can help measure the success of blind hiring techniques.

In conclusion, blind hiring methods can be a good way to get rid of unconscious bias during the hiring process. Hiring managers can evaluate candidates based on their skills and qualifications if they take out personal information from their applications and use skills-based tests. However, blind hiring techniques should be used in conjunction with other diversity recruiting strategies and may not be suitable for all types of roles. Measuring the effectiveness of blind hiring techniques can be challenging but establishing metrics before implementation can help track progress.

CHAPTER 6: TRAINING HIRING MANAGERS ON DIVERSITY AND INCLUSION

Hiring managers oversee finding the best people for open jobs, interviewing them, and choosing the best ones. To create a diverse and welcoming workplace, it is important for hiring managers to know and follow best practices for diversity and inclusion. This includes making plans to attract and keep a diverse pool of talent, finding and getting rid of unconscious bias, and promoting a workplace culture that welcomes everyone.

In this chapter, we'll talk about why diversity and inclusion training for hiring managers is so important. We'll provide tips for developing and implementing training programs, as well as examples of successful training initiatives.

I. Why Training Hiring Managers on Diversity and Inclusion is Important

- Hiring managers are often the first point of contact for job applicants and have a significant impact on the candidate experience. Research shows that unconscious bias can impact hiring decisions, leading to a less diverse and inclusive workplace. By training hiring managers on diversity and inclusion best practices, organizations can improve their hiring processes and attract a more diverse pool of candidates.

- In addition, training hiring managers can help promote an inclusive workplace culture. When managers understand and value diversity, they are better equipped to create an environment where all employees feel respected and included. This can lead to improved employee morale, increased retention, and a stronger employer brand.

II.   **Key considerations to keep in mind when developing a diversity and inclusion training program for hiring managers.**

- Assess the current state of diversity and inclusion in your organization. Before developing a training program, it is important to understand the current state of diversity and inclusion in your organization. This can involve gathering data on the demographic makeup of your workforce as well as conducting surveys or focus groups to assess employee perceptions of the workplace climate.

- Define the learning objectives of the training program. What do you want hiring managers to learn and be able to do after completing the training program? Consider the specific skills and knowledge areas that are most relevant to your organization, such as identifying and mitigating unconscious bias or building diverse talent pipelines.

- Select appropriate training methods. There are many different training methods that can be used to deliver diversity and inclusion training, including online modules, in-person workshops, and coaching. Consider the learning preferences of your audience, as well as the resources and time available for training.

- Engage subject-matter experts. Consider partnering with external consultants or internal subject-matter experts to help develop and deliver the training program. These individuals can bring valuable insights and perspectives to the program and help ensure that it is tailored to the specific needs of your organization.

- Incorporate ongoing evaluation and feedback. It is important to evaluate the effectiveness of the training program and gather feedback from participants to identify areas for improvement. Consider using surveys, focus groups, or other evaluation methods to assess the impact of the training on hiring managers' skills and behaviors.

Many organizations have developed successful diversity and inclusion training programs for hiring managers. Here are a few examples:

Intel has developed a comprehensive diversity and inclusion training program for its hiring managers, which includes modules on unconscious bias, inclusive hiring practices, and building diverse teams. The program is delivered through a combination of in-person and online training, and participants are required to complete the training before making hiring decisions.

LinkedIn has developed a training program for its recruiting team that focuses on building diverse talent pipelines. The program includes modules on sourcing and outreach strategies as well as the importance of inclusive language in job postings.

Google has implemented a training program for its hiring managers that focuses on identifying and mitigating unconscious bias. The program includes online modules, in-person workshops, and coaching and is designed to help managers make fair and equitable hiring decisions.

Note that it is important to involve all levels of management in the training process. Training programs should not only be limited to hiring managers but also extend to other stakeholders, such as recruiters and HR professionals. Providing a comprehensive training program that includes everyone involved in the recruitment process and management of the organization can help ensure that diversity and inclusion are part of the organizational culture and not just a checkbox to be ticked.

It is also important to make training programs interactive and engaging. Simply providing information through lectures or online modules may not be effective. Instead, training programs should incorporate activities that allow participants to practice and apply what they have learned. Role-playing exercises, case studies, and group discussions can be effective methods for engaging participants and reinforcing learning.

Measuring the effectiveness of training programs is also critical. Organizations should establish metrics to evaluate the impact of the training on recruitment and retention rates of diverse candidates. Surveys, focus groups, and performance metrics can be used to gather data on the effectiveness of the training programs.

Overall, training hiring managers on diversity and inclusion is a crucial step towards creating a diverse and inclusive workplace. By providing comprehensive and interactive training programs, organizations can equip their hiring managers with the skills and knowledge needed to attract and retain diverse talent. Measuring the effectiveness of these programs can help ensure that they are making a tangible impact on the recruitment and retention of diverse candidates.

Training hiring managers on diversity and inclusion is essential to ensuring they have the knowledge and skills needed to create an inclusive workplace. However, training should not be a one-time event but an ongoing process. It is essential to provide regular training and resources to hiring managers to ensure they are up to date with the latest best practices and policies. Training can include workshops, online courses, and resources such as diversity and inclusion toolkits.

Additionally, it is crucial to evaluate the effectiveness of training programs regularly. Feedback and metrics can be used to measure the impact of training on hiring practices and diversity outcomes. The goal is to create a continuous learning culture that prioritizes diversity and inclusion.

CHAPTER 7: MEASURING DIVERSITY RECRUITMENT SUCCESS

Measuring the success of diversity recruiting efforts is a key part of making sure that an organization is building a workforce that is diverse and welcomes everyone. Without keeping track of and analyzing relevant data, it can be hard to figure out how well recruitment strategies work and where they can be improved. In this chapter, we'll look at how to measure the success of hiring people from different backgrounds and talk about the key metrics that organizations should keep track of.

I.   Key Metrics for Measuring Diversity Recruitment Success

To measure the success of diversity recruiting efforts, organizations should track a range of metrics that capture different aspects of the recruitment process. Some of the key metrics to consider include:

- **Diversity of Applicant Pool:** Tracking the diversity of the applicant pool can help organizations determine whether they are attracting a diverse range of candidates. This metric could include information on the gender, race, ethnicity, and other dimensions of diversity of applicants.

- **Diversity of Hires:** The diversity of hires is another critical metric to track. This metric measures the percentage of new hires who belong to underrepresented groups. This metric is crucial to determining whether the recruitment process is resulting in a diverse workforce.

- **Time-to-Fill:** Time-to-fill is the length of time it takes to fill a position. Tracking this metric can help organizations identify any bottlenecks or inefficiencies in the recruitment process.

- **Offer Acceptance Rate:** The offer acceptance rate is the percentage of job offers that are accepted. A low offer acceptance rate could indicate that there are issues with the recruitment process or that candidates are not being offered competitive compensation packages.

- **Retention Rate:** Retention rate measures the percentage of employees who stay with the organization for a specific period. Tracking this metric can help organizations determine whether they are effectively retaining diverse talent.

- **Employee Engagement:** Employee engagement measures the level of commitment, motivation, and satisfaction of employees. Tracking this metric can help organizations determine whether their diversity initiatives are positively impacting the workplace culture and employee morale.

II. Collecting and Analyzing Data:

Collecting and analyzing data is critical to measuring the success of diversity recruitment initiatives. Organizations should develop a data collection strategy that includes both quantitative and qualitative data. Some best practices for data collection and analysis include the following:

- **Use of Applicant Tracking Systems (ATS):** ATS can help organizations track key recruitment metrics such as the diversity of the applicant pool, time-to-fill, and offer acceptance rate.

- **Surveys and Feedback:** Surveys and feedback from candidates, employees, and hiring managers can provide valuable qualitative data on the effectiveness of diversity recruitment initiatives.

- **Regular Reporting:** Regular reporting on key metrics can help organizations identify trends and areas for improvement. Reports should be easily accessible and shared with relevant stakeholders.

- **Benchmarking:** Benchmarking against industry standards and best practices can help organizations determine how they compare to other organizations and identify opportunities for improvement.

III. Using Data to Improve Recruitment Efforts

Once organizations have collected and analyzed relevant data, they should use this information to make data-driven decisions and improve recruitment efforts. Some strategies for using data to improve recruitment efforts include:

- **Adjusting Recruitment Strategies:** Organizations should use data to identify areas where recruitment efforts are falling short and adjust strategies accordingly. For example, if the diversity of the applicant pool is low, organizations may need to expand sourcing channels or improve job descriptions to attract a more diverse range of candidates.

- **Providing Training and Support:** Data can help organizations identify areas where hiring managers may need additional support or training. For example, if data shows that hiring managers are not effectively evaluating candidates based on skills and experience; organizations can provide training on unbiased hiring practices.

- **Celebrating Success:** Celebrating successes and publicly acknowledging improvements can help motivate employees and maintain momentum for diversity recruitment initiatives.

To determine which metrics to track, it's important to first define specific diversity recruitment goals. These goals can include increasing the representation of underrepresented groups in the candidate pool or improving the diversity of new hires. Once the goals are identified, metrics can be chosen that align with them.

Some common metrics that organizations track to measure diversity recruitment success include:

- **Diversity of candidate pool:** This metric measures the diversity of applicants for a particular position or across all positions. Organizations can track the percentage of candidates from underrepresented groups in the pool as well as the overall diversity of the pool.

- **Diversity of new hires:** This metric measures the diversity of individuals who are hired. Organizations can track the percentage of new hires from underrepresented groups as well as the overall diversity of new hires.

- **Time-to-fill:** This metric measures the amount of time it takes to fill a position. Tracking time-to-fill for diverse candidates can help identify areas where the recruitment process may be stalling or where changes may need to be made to attract a more diverse pool of candidates.

- **Candidate experience:** This metric measures the experience that candidates have during the recruitment process. Organizations can track candidate satisfaction with the recruitment process as well as their perceptions of the organization's commitment to diversity and inclusion.

- **Retention:** This metric measures the retention of diverse hires. Organizations can track the retention rate of diverse hires compared to the retention rate of non-diverse hires.

In addition to tracking these metrics, it's important to analyze the data and use it to improve recruitment efforts. For example, if the diversity of the candidate pool is low, organizations may need to adjust their sourcing channels or outreach efforts to attract a more diverse pool of candidates. If the retention rate of diverse hires is lower than that of non-diverse hires, organizations may need to focus on improving their retention strategies for diverse employees.

Overall, measuring diversity recruitment success requires a commitment to data collection and analysis. By tracking the right metrics and using data to drive decision-making, organizations can ensure that they are making progress toward their diversity goals.

To make a diverse and inclusive workforce, it's important to measure how well diversity recruitment programs work. Organizations can make sure they are attracting and keeping top talent from a wide range of backgrounds by keeping track of key metrics and using data to guide recruitment strategies. It is important to regularly review and adjust diversity recruitment strategies to ensure they are effective and meet the goals of the organization. By implementing the strategies discussed in this guide, organizations can develop a diverse talent pipeline and foster a culture of inclusion that benefits everyone in the workplace. With a commitment to diversity and inclusion, organizations can create a stronger and more successful business over the long term.

CHAPTER 8: LEVERAGING EMPLOYEE REFERRAL PROGRAMS FOR DIVERSITY RECRUITMENT

Employee referral programs have become a popular method for companies to attract new talent. In fact, studies have shown that employee referrals are the most effective source of new hires. However, relying solely on employee referrals may result in a lack of diversity in the workforce, as employees tend to refer candidates who are like themselves. Therefore, it is important to leverage employee referral programs for diversity recruitment. In this chapter, we will explore how to develop and implement effective employee referral programs that promote diversity.

I.   Why Employee Referral Programs

Employee referral programs are a popular and cost-effective method for recruiting new talent. They involve incentivizing current employees to refer their friends, family, or acquaintances for open job positions. Employee referrals are considered a great source of new hires because they often result in a higher retention rate and better cultural fit. Additionally, employees tend to refer candidates who are a good match for the company culture and who have similar work ethics and values.

But relying only on employee referrals can lead to a workforce with too few different kinds of people. Employees tend to refer candidates who are like themselves, which can lead to a lack of diversity in terms of race, gender, ethnicity, and other demographics. Therefore, it is important to leverage employee referral programs for diversity recruitment.

II.   Developing a Diversity-Focused Employee Referral Program

To develop a successful employee referral program that promotes diversity, companies need to take specific steps. Below are some key considerations to keep in mind:

- **Define Diversity Goals**

The first step in developing a diversity-focused employee referral program is to define diversity goals. Companies should establish specific goals for diversity recruitment and outline the metrics they will use to measure progress. For example, a company may set a goal to increase the percentage of women in leadership positions by a certain percentage over a specified period of time.

- **Communicate the Importance of Diversity**

It is essential to communicate the importance of diversity to employees and encourage them to participate in the program. Companies should make it clear that diversity is a top priority and that they are committed to creating a more inclusive workforce. Communication can take the form of company-wide announcements, newsletters, and training sessions.

- **Provide Training**

Training is an essential component of a successful employee referral program. Employees should be trained on the importance of diversity, how to identify potential candidates from diverse backgrounds, and how to make referrals. Additionally, training should include information on unconscious bias and how to avoid it in the referral process.

- **Incentivize Referrals**

To encourage employees to participate in the program, companies should provide incentives for successful referrals. Incentives can take the form of cash bonuses, paid time off, or other rewards. However, it is important to ensure that incentives are fair and equitable and that all employees have an equal opportunity to participate.

- **Use Inclusive Language in Referral Materials**

Using inclusive language in referral materials can help attract a more diverse pool of candidates. Referral materials should avoid language that could be perceived as discriminatory and should be designed to appeal to a diverse range of candidates.

- **Track Diversity Metrics**

To measure the success of the employee referral program, companies should track diversity metrics. This includes tracking the demographics of referred candidates and the number of referrals made by employees from underrepresented groups. By tracking these metrics, companies can identify areas where they need to improve and adjust their approach accordingly.

III. Examples of Successful Employee Referral Programs

Several companies have developed successful employee referral programs that promote diversity. Below are some examples:

- **Intel:** Intel has implemented a successful employee referral program that includes a diversity-focused approach. The program includes a diversity bonus for referrals that result in the hiring of underrepresented candidates. Additionally, Intel has developed a referral portal that allows employees to search for and refer candidates from underrepresented groups.

- **Salesforce:** Salesforce has a successful employee referral program that emphasizes diversity and inclusion. The company offers bonuses to employees who refer diverse candidates, defined as women, people of color, LGBTQ+ individuals, veterans, and people with disabilities. They also have a diversity recruiting team dedicated to sourcing candidates from underrepresented groups and ensuring they are included in the referral program. By prioritizing diversity in their referral program, **Salesforce** has increased the diversity of their workforce and created a more inclusive workplace culture.

Another way to encourage diversity in employee referral programs is to give employees a reason to recommend people from different backgrounds. This can be done by offering a higher bonus for referring a candidate from an underrepresented group. Also, organizations can host events that focus on diversity, like a panel for women in leadership or a job fair for people of different backgrounds, to get employees to network and recommend diverse candidates.

It is also essential to ensure that the referral process is accessible to all employees. Some employees may not have a large network or may not feel comfortable referring candidates. Therefore, organizations should provide resources and support to help employees make referrals. This can include training on diversity and inclusion, providing sample job descriptions and outreach messages, and offering a referral hotline or email address for employees who may not have a direct referral.

To measure the effectiveness of employee referral programs, organizations should track metrics such as the number of referrals, the diversity of referred candidates, and the percentage of referrals that result in hires. This data can help organizations identify areas for improvement and adjust their referral programs accordingly. Organizations should also regularly review and update their referral programs to ensure they are effective in attracting and retaining a diverse workforce.

Employee referral programs can be a great way for a company to promote diversity and inclusion. By putting in place strategies to encourage referrals of diverse candidates, giving employees the support and tools they need to make referrals, and measuring how well the program is working, organizations can build a strong pipeline of diverse talent and make the workplace more welcoming for everyone.

CHAPTER 9: CREATING A DIVERSITY-FOCUSED CANDIDATE EXPERIENCE

Organizations that want to attract and keep diverse talent need to make sure the candidate experience is positive and welcoming. The candidate experience is all a candidate's interactions with a company during the hiring process, from the first job posting to the final hiring decision. It is important to make sure that these interactions promote diversity and inclusion and make a place where candidates from all backgrounds feel welcome. In this chapter, we'll talk about how to create a candidate experience that is focused on diversity and helps organizations find and keep diverse talent.

I.   Communicating   an   Organization's   Commitment   to Diversity

The first step in creating a diversity-focused candidate experience is to communicate an organization's commitment to diversity and inclusion. This can be done through various channels, such as the organization's website, social media, and job postings. It is essential to use language that reflects the organization's commitment to diversity and inclusion and to highlight any diversity initiatives or programs that the organization has in place. For example, an organization could include a statement on its website that emphasizes its commitment to creating a diverse and inclusive workplace and mentions any diversity initiatives or programs that the organization has implemented.

II.   Creating an Inclusive Job Posting

Job postings are often the first point of contact that candidates have with an organization, and they can have a significant impact on the diversity of the candidate pool. Therefore, it is essential to create inclusive job postings that attract candidates from all backgrounds. Inclusive job postings should use gender-neutral language and avoid language that may be perceived as discriminatory or exclusionary. For example, using terms like "rockstar" or "ninja" to describe job requirements can discourage qualified candidates who may not identify with these terms. Additionally, job postings should focus on essential skills and qualifications, rather than unnecessary or arbitrary requirements that may exclude qualified candidates.

III.   Ensuring a Fair and Equitable Recruitment Process

Creating a diversity-focused candidate experience also means ensuring that the recruitment process is fair and equitable for all candidates. This includes providing equal opportunities for all candidates to showcase their skills and abilities, regardless of their background. For example, interview questions should focus on skills and qualifications rather than personal characteristics or demographic information. Additionally, it is essential to ensure that all candidates have access to the same resources and support throughout the recruitment process. This may include providing accommodations for candidates with disabilities or ensuring that all candidates have access to the same information and resources.

IV.   Involving Diverse Employees in the Recruitment Process

Involving diverse employees in the recruitment process can help create a more inclusive candidate experience. Diverse employees can provide valuable insights into the recruitment process and help identify potential biases or barriers that may discourage diverse candidates from applying. Additionally, diverse employees can serve as ambassadors for the organization, helping to attract diverse talent and promote the organization's commitment to diversity and inclusion. Involving diverse employees in the recruitment process may include inviting them to participate in the interview process, providing feedback on job postings, or asking for their input on recruitment initiatives and strategies.

V.   Providing Feedback and Follow-Up

Providing feedback and follow-up is an essential component of creating a positive candidate experience. Candidates who apply for a job and do not hear back from the organization may be discouraged from applying again in the future or may form a negative impression of the organization. Therefore, it is essential to provide timely feedback and follow-up to all candidates, regardless of whether they are ultimately hired. This includes providing constructive feedback on areas for improvement and ensuring that candidates feel valued and respected throughout the recruitment process.

Creating a diverse candidate experience starts with ensuring that job postings and application processes are inclusive. Job descriptions should use inclusive language that welcomes applicants from all backgrounds. Application forms should be accessible and easy to navigate, avoiding any unnecessary or irrelevant questions. Additionally, it's important to ensure that candidates receive timely and respectful communication throughout the recruitment process, regardless of whether they are ultimately hired.

Another key aspect of the candidate experience is providing opportunities for candidates to learn more about the organization's commitment to diversity and inclusion. This can include providing information on the organization's diversity initiatives and employee resource groups (ERGs). ERGs are employee-led groups that promote diversity and inclusion within an organization. By showcasing these initiatives, candidates can gain a better understanding of the organization's values and culture.

Organizations can also provide opportunities for candidates to interact with current employees from diverse backgrounds. This can include organizing networking events or panel discussions featuring employees from ERGs. These interactions can provide candidates with a sense of the organization's culture and values, as well as opportunities to ask questions and learn more about the organization.

It's important to ensure that the recruitment process is fair and equitable. This means providing equal opportunities for all candidates and eliminating any unconscious bias in the selection process. Blind hiring techniques, such as removing identifying information from applications, can help eliminate bias. Additionally, providing diversity and inclusion training for hiring managers can help ensure that they are equipped with the skills and knowledge to conduct a fair and unbiased recruitment process.

By creating a diverse and inclusive candidate experience, organizations can attract and retain diverse talent. Candidates are more likely to consider organizations that prioritize diversity and inclusion, and providing a positive candidate experience can help organizations stand out in a competitive job market.

Creating a diversity-focused candidate experience is essential for organizations looking to attract and retain diverse talent. By communicating an organization's commitment to diversity and inclusion, creating inclusive job postings, ensuring a fair and equitable recruitment process, involving diverse employees, and providing feedback and follow-up, organizations can create a positive and inclusive candidate experience that promotes diversity and inclusion.

CHAPTER 10: RETAINING DIVERSE TALENT

Hiring diverse talent is just the first step in building a diverse and inclusive workforce. Retaining that talent is equally important. In this chapter, we will discuss strategies for retaining diverse talent and creating a workplace culture that is inclusive and supportive. We will explore best practices for providing professional development opportunities, creating a sense of belonging, and promoting growth and advancement.

I.   Creating a Culture of Inclusion

One of the most important factors in retaining diverse talent is creating a culture of inclusion. Employees need to feel valued and supported to thrive in their roles. Organizations should foster a culture that embraces diversity and encourages employees to bring their whole selves to work. This can be achieved by promoting open communication, recognizing and celebrating differences, and creating opportunities for employees to connect and engage with each other.

II. Professional Development Opportunities

Providing professional development opportunities is also critical to retaining diverse talent. Employees want to feel that they are growing and advancing in their careers. Organizations should offer training and development programs that are tailored to the needs and goals of diverse employees. This can include mentorship programs, leadership development, and access to training and certifications.

III. Sense of Belonging

Creating a sense of belonging is also crucial to retaining diverse talent. Employees want to feel that they belong and are part of the organization. This can be achieved by providing opportunities for employees to connect with each other and the broader community. This can include employee resource groups, volunteering opportunities, and community outreach programs.

IV. Promoting Growth and Advancement

Finally, organizations should promote growth and advancement opportunities for diverse talent. Employees want to know that there are opportunities for advancement and that their contributions are valued. Organizations should offer clear career paths and promotion opportunities, as well as recognize and reward employees for their accomplishments. This can include regular performance reviews, promotions, and bonuses.

V. Case Study:

Netflix is a company that has made diversity and inclusion a priority in their recruitment and retention strategies. They have implemented several initiatives to create a culture of inclusion and support the growth and advancement of diverse employees.

One of Netflix's key strategies for retaining diverse talent is to provide opportunities for employees to grow and advance in their careers. They offer a range of training and development programs, including leadership development, mentorship, and access to training and certifications.

Netflix also recognizes the importance of creating a sense of belonging for diverse employees. They have established employee resource groups that provide opportunities for employees to connect with each other and engage with the broader community. They also offer volunteer opportunities and community outreach programs.

Another key strategy for retaining diverse talent at Netflix is recognizing and rewarding employees for their accomplishments. They offer regular performance reviews and promotions, as well as bonuses and equity awards for exceptional performance.

Another effective retention strategy is to provide regular feedback and performance evaluations to employees. This feedback can help employees understand their strengths and areas for improvement and allow them to take ownership of their career development. It is essential to ensure that the evaluation process is objective and free from unconscious bias to promote a fair and equitable workplace.

Another critical aspect of retaining diverse talent is providing opportunities for growth and advancement. Organizations can offer professional development programs, mentoring, and coaching to support employees' growth and career advancement. These programs should be available to all employees, regardless of their background or identity, to promote an inclusive workplace.

Creating a culture of inclusion is crucial to retaining diverse talent. Employees want to feel valued and included in the workplace, and organizations should strive to create an environment where everyone feels welcome and respected. Encouraging diversity and inclusion at all levels of the organization can help foster a sense of belonging and make employees feel valued and supported.

Organizations can consider offering diversity and inclusion training to their employees. This training can help employees develop the skills and knowledge needed to work effectively with colleagues from diverse backgrounds and promote a more inclusive workplace culture.

Retaining diverse talent is a critical component of diversity recruiting efforts. By developing retention strategies that promote growth, advancement, and inclusion, organizations can ensure that their diverse talent feels valued and supported. Creating a culture of inclusion and providing opportunities for professional development can go a long way toward retaining diverse talent and building a diverse and inclusive workforce.

Retaining diverse talent is critical to building a diverse and inclusive workforce. Organizations should focus on creating a culture of inclusion, providing professional development opportunities, promoting a sense of belonging, and offering growth and advancement opportunities. By implementing these strategies, organizations can create an environment that supports the retention of diverse talent and promotes their ongoing success and growth.

CHAPTER 11: BUILDING A DIVERSE LEADERSHIP PIPELINE

A diverse leadership pipeline is essential for organizations that want to promote a culture of inclusion and equity. A diverse leadership team brings different perspectives, experiences, and backgrounds to decision-making processes, which can lead to innovation and better business outcomes. But it can be hard to build a diverse leadership pipeline because biases and structural barriers can stop people from different backgrounds from getting to leadership positions. In this chapter, we will discuss strategies for identifying and developing diverse talent for leadership roles, as well as ways to promote diversity in executive search firms and boardrooms.

I.   Identifying Diverse Talent for Leadership Roles

To build a diverse leadership pipeline, organizations must first identify diverse talent within their ranks. However, identifying diverse talent can be challenging, as bias and structural barriers may prevent diverse employees from advancing to leadership positions. To overcome these challenges, organizations can implement the following strategies:

- **Foster a Culture of Inclusion:** A culture of inclusion is essential to ensuring that all employees have an equal opportunity to advance to leadership positions. By creating a workplace culture that values diversity and equity, organizations can attract and retain diverse talent, which can help build a diverse leadership pipeline.

- **Develop a succession planning process:** Succession planning is the process of identifying and developing employees for future leadership roles. By developing a succession planning process that includes diverse candidates, organizations can ensure that diverse talent is considered for leadership positions.

- **Use data to identify potential leaders:** Using data analytics tools, organizations can identify employees who have the potential to become leaders. Data such as performance metrics, career aspirations, and employee feedback can help identify diverse talent that may not be immediately visible.

- **Encourage employee referrals:** Employee referral programs can be an effective way to identify diverse talent for leadership positions. By encouraging employees to refer diverse candidates, organizations can tap into networks that may be inaccessible through traditional recruiting methods.

II.   Developing Diverse Leaders

Once diverse talent has been identified, organizations must develop and prepare them for leadership positions. This can be accomplished through the following strategies:

- **Leadership Development Programs:** Leadership development programs can provide diverse talent with the skills and knowledge needed to succeed in leadership roles. These programs can include training in areas such as communication, strategic thinking, and decision-making.

- **Mentoring and coaching:** Mentoring and coaching can be effective ways to develop diverse talent for leadership positions. By pairing diverse employees with experienced mentors, organizations can provide them with the support and guidance needed to succeed in leadership roles.

- **Assign high-profile projects:** Assigning diverse talent to high-profile projects can provide them with the opportunity to showcase their skills and abilities. This can help build their confidence and increase their visibility within the organization.

- **Provide feedback and support:** Providing regular feedback and support to diverse employees can help them develop the skills and knowledge needed to succeed in leadership roles. Feedback can include areas for improvement and strengths, and support can include resources such as training and development opportunities.

III.   Promoting Diversity in Executive Search Firms and Boardrooms

To ensure that diverse talent is considered for leadership roles, organizations must also promote diversity in executive search firms and boardrooms. This can be accomplished through the following strategies:

- **Use executive search firms that focus on diversity:** Executive search firms that specialize in diversity and inclusion can help organizations identify and attract diverse candidates for leadership positions.

- **Develop relationships with diverse professional associations:** Building relationships with diverse professional associations can provide organizations with access to a pool of diverse candidates for leadership positions.

- **Require diversity on boards:** Requiring diversity on boards can ensure that diverse perspectives are represented in decision-making processes. This can include requirements for gender, race, ethnicity, and other diversity dimensions.

- **Provide diversity training for search committees:** Providing diversity training for search committees can help ensure that they are aware of their biases and are actively seeking diverse candidates.

Creating opportunities for career growth and advancement is another way to build a pipeline of leaders from different backgrounds. Organizations can implement mentorship programs, coaching sessions, and leadership training programs to support the development of diverse talent. This helps to address the leadership gap that can occur when diverse talent is not given the same opportunities for growth and advancement as their non-diverse counterparts.

Organizations can prioritize diverse representation in executive search firms and boardrooms. When selecting search firms, it is important to choose those that prioritize diversity and inclusion in their recruitment efforts. The same goes for selecting board members who can bring diverse perspectives and experiences to the table. Board diversity has been shown to lead to better decision-making and improved financial performance, making it a win-win for the organization.

Organizations must hold themselves accountable for their diversity and inclusion efforts. This means setting goals and regularly measuring progress towards those goals. Leaders must take ownership of creating a diverse and inclusive culture and hold themselves and their teams accountable for meeting diversity goals. By building a diverse leadership pipeline, organizations can ensure that they have the talent and perspectives needed to drive success in their diversity and inclusion efforts.

Building a diverse leadership pipeline is critical for ensuring an organization's success in diversity and inclusion. This requires a commitment from leadership to prioritize diversity in all aspects of the organization, from recruitment to career development to executive search firms and boardrooms. By implementing strategies for identifying and developing diverse talent, providing opportunities for growth and advancement, and holding themselves accountable for progress, organizations can build a strong and diverse leadership pipeline that will drive success in their diversity and inclusion efforts.

CHAPTER 12: OVERCOMING DIVERSITY RECRUITING CHALLENGES

While diversity recruiting has numerous benefits, it is not without its challenges. Organizations may face various obstacles in their efforts to attract and retain diverse talent. These challenges can range from unconscious bias to legal and regulatory requirements. It is essential for organizations to identify and address these challenges to create a truly diverse and inclusive workforce. In this chapter, we will explore some common diversity recruiting challenges and provide strategies for overcoming them.

I.   Unconscious Bias

Unconscious bias can be a significant barrier to diverse recruiting. Unconscious bias refers to the unconscious stereotypes and attitudes that people hold about others based on factors such as race, gender, and age. These biases can affect the way that recruiters evaluate candidates and can lead to the exclusion of qualified candidates from diverse backgrounds.

To overcome unconscious bias in recruiting, organizations can implement blind hiring techniques, such as removing identifying information from candidate applications. Additionally, training recruiters and hiring managers on diversity and inclusion best practices can help them become more aware of their biases and make more objective hiring decisions. Organizations can also conduct regular audits of their hiring processes to identify and address any potential biases.

II.   Resistance to Change

Resistance to change can also be a challenge in diversity recruiting. Some individuals may be resistant to change and may not see the value of diversity in the workplace. This resistance can manifest in various ways, such as reluctance to adopt new hiring practices or pushback against diversity initiatives.

To overcome resistance to change, it is essential to communicate the value of diversity and inclusion clearly. This can include sharing data on the benefits of a diverse workforce, such as increased innovation and better financial performance. Additionally, involving key stakeholders, such as managers and employees, in the diversity recruitment process can help build buy-in and support for diversity initiatives.

III.   Legal and Regulatory Requirements

Legal and regulatory requirements can also pose a challenge in diversity recruiting. Organizations must comply with laws and regulations related to equal employment opportunity and affirmative action. Failure to comply with these requirements can result in legal and financial consequences.

To overcome legal and regulatory challenges in diversity recruiting, it is essential to have a clear understanding of the laws and regulations that apply to your organization. Organizations can work with legal counsel or compliance experts to ensure that they are in compliance with all relevant laws and regulations. Additionally, organizations can conduct regular audits of their hiring processes to identify any potential compliance issues.

IV. Adapting to Changing Demographics

As the demographics of the workforce and society continue to shift, organizations must adapt their diversity recruiting strategies to meet these changes. This may involve understanding and catering to the needs and preferences of different generations, cultures, and backgrounds, as well as identifying new and emerging talent sources.

V. Measuring the Impact of Diversity Recruiting

Measuring the impact of diversity recruiting can be a challenge, but it is essential to understand the effectiveness of the strategies and make necessary adjustments. Organizations should regularly track and analyze data on diversity recruiting metrics, such as candidate demographics, hiring rates, retention rates, and promotions, and use this information to make data-driven decisions about their diversity recruiting initiatives.

Diversity recruiting can be a challenging but rewarding process. By addressing challenges such as unconscious bias, resistance to change, and legal and regulatory requirements, organizations can create a more diverse and inclusive workforce. It is essential to remain committed to diversity and inclusion efforts and to continually evaluate and improve recruitment strategies. By doing so, organizations can reap the benefits of a diverse workforce, including increased innovation, better financial performance, and a more positive company culture.

CONCLUSION:

In this book, we have explored powerful diversity recruiting strategies to fuel talent pipeline. Building a diverse workforce is not only the right thing to do but also a smart business strategy. By following the strategies and best practices outlined in this book, organizations can attract and retain top talent from diverse backgrounds, resulting in increased innovation, productivity, and profitability.

By implementing diversity recruiting strategies, organizations can enhance their reputation as an employer of choice, attracting more diverse talent and creating a positive brand image. It is important to remember that diversity recruiting is an ongoing process, and organizations must continuously assess and improve their strategies to ensure they are meeting their diversity and inclusion goals.

While there may be challenges and obstacles to overcome, including unconscious bias and resistance to change, organizations can overcome these barriers by prioritizing diversity and inclusion at all levels of the organization. Additionally, by tracking and measuring key metrics, organizations can ensure that their diversity recruiting efforts are effective and adjust their strategies accordingly.

Ultimately, building a diverse workforce requires a commitment to creating a culture of inclusion where all employees feel valued and respected. By promoting diversity and inclusion, organizations can unlock the full potential of their workforce, leading to long-term success and sustainable growth.

It is also important to remember that diversity and inclusion efforts are not a one-time fix but rather an ongoing process that requires commitment and dedication. Organizations must continuously assess and adjust their diversity and inclusion strategies to ensure they are effective and aligned with their goals.

It is also important to note that diversity recruiting is just one piece of the puzzle in creating a truly diverse and inclusive workplace. Organizations must also focus on creating an inclusive culture that values and respects differences, provides equal opportunities for growth and development, and holds all employees accountable for promoting diversity and inclusion.

Finally, it is important to acknowledge that there are still significant challenges and barriers to achieving diversity and inclusion in the workplace, including systemic inequality and unconscious bias. However, with a commitment to ongoing learning and improvement, organizations can continue to make progress towards creating a more diverse and inclusive workplace for all.

PRACTICAL EXERCISES

Here are some talent diversity and inclusion management exercises for hiring managers:

Role-Playing Exercises: Conduct role-playing exercises with hiring managers to simulate real-world scenarios where diversity and inclusion are critical. For example, you can create a scenario where a hiring manager has to choose between two candidates with similar qualifications but different backgrounds. This activity can help people in charge of hiring understand how unconscious biases can affect how they make decisions.

Collaborative hiring: Tell hiring managers to work with their peers from other departments to make sure that the hiring process takes into account different points of view and experiences. Consider putting together a diversity and inclusion task force to oversee the hiring process and make sure that hiring managers follow best practices and company policies.

Training and development: Help hiring managers understand the importance of diversity and inclusion in the workplace by giving them training and development opportunities. This can be done by going to workshops, seminars, or online courses that focus on diversity, equity, and inclusion. Giving hiring managers ongoing training can also help to show how important these values are and keep them up to date on the latest trends and best practices in managing talent for diversity and inclusion.

Conduct a diversity self-assessment: Have the hiring managers reflect on their personal biases and assumptions towards different demographics. This can be done through a series of questions, such as "What stereotypes do you hold about certain groups of people?" or "What unconscious biases may be influencing your hiring decisions?" or "How do you approach diversity when it comes to recruiting candidates?"

Evaluate job descriptions for bias: Provide the hiring managers with a list of words or phrases that could be interpreted as biased towards certain groups, such as "strong leadership skills" or "able to work in a fast-paced environment". Ask them to look over job descriptions and change any biased language they find with language that is more inclusive and neutral.

Create diverse candidate pools: Encourage hiring managers to look beyond their usual sources for candidates and explore new channels for recruiting talent. This could include attending job fairs at historically Black colleges and universities, partnering with disability organizations, or posting job openings on websites and forums that cater to diverse communities.

Conduct inclusive interviews: Train hiring managers to conduct inclusive interviews by asking open-ended questions that allow candidates to showcase their skills and experiences. This includes avoiding questions that may be culturally insensitive or biased, such as asking a candidate about their accent or national origin.

Establish mentorship programs: Help hiring managers develop mentorship programs that provide support and guidance to underrepresented employees in the organization. This can include pairing employees with mentors from different backgrounds, hosting diversity and inclusion workshops, or creating affinity groups where employees can connect and share their experiences.

By engaging in these exercises, hiring managers can become more mindful of their own biases and behaviors, which can ultimately lead to a more diverse and inclusive workplace.

REFERENCE LIST:

Adams, M. (2017). The Inclusive Leader: An Applied Approach to Diversity, Change, and Management. Routledge.

Gardner, H. (2011). Frames of Mind: The Theory of Multiple Intelligences. Basic Books.

Hewlett, S. A. (2013). Forget a Mentor, Find a Sponsor: The New Way to Fast-Track Your Career. Harvard Business Review Press.

Johnson, J. F. (2017). Privilege, Power, and Difference. McGraw-Hill Education.

Llopis, G. (2015). The Three Keys to Success: Unlocking the Power of the Three Human Capacities. Forbes.

Martin, R. (2014). Yes, You Can Measure Diversity. Harvard Business Review.

Nelson, B. (2018). The Leadership Gap: What Gets Between You and Your Greatness. Penguin.

Page, S. E. (2007). The Difference: How the Power of Diversity Creates Better Groups, Firms, Schools, and Societies. Princeton University Press.

Robinson, V. M. (2008). Leading People: The 8 Proven Principles for Success in Business. Pearson Education.

Scott, S. (2018). Inclusion: Diversity, the New Workplace, and the Will to Change. Hachette Books.

Dear Friend,

As you come to the end of this book, I hope you have gained valuable insights into the power of diversity recruiting and how it can help you build a more inclusive and successful organization.

Remember that diversity and inclusion are not just buzzwords but essential components of a thriving workplace. By embracing diverse perspectives, experiences, and backgrounds, you can create a culture of innovation and creativity that drives your business forward.

I want to thank you for joining us on this journey, and I hope that the strategies and techniques shared in this book will inspire you to take action and make a positive impact on your organization.

Best wishes,
Felix Tih

GLOSSARY

Diversity: The practice of actively seeking, welcoming, and including individuals from a wide range of backgrounds, experiences, and perspectives.

Inclusion: The practice of ensuring that all individuals, regardless of their background or identity, are valued, respected, and given equal opportunities to participate and contribute to the organization.

Talent pipeline: A talent pipeline is a pool of candidates who are ready to fill a position.The process of identifying, attracting, and developing potential candidates for future job openings within an organization.

Recruiting: The process of attracting and selecting qualified candidates for job openings within an organization.

Candidate experience: The overall impression and perception that a job candidate has of an organization and its hiring process.

Employer branding: The process of promoting an organization as an attractive employer to potential job candidates and the public.

Implicit bias: Unconscious attitudes or stereotypes that affect our perceptions, decisions, and behaviors, often without our awareness.

Diversity and inclusion training: Programs designed to increase awareness and understanding of diversity issues and provide skills and strategies for promoting an inclusive workplace culture.

Affirmative action: Policies and programs that promote the hiring and advancement of individuals from historically underrepresented groups, such as women and minorities.

Metrics: Quantitative data and measurements used to evaluate the effectiveness and impact of diversity recruiting strategies and initiatives.

Affirmative action: Policies or programs designed to address discrimination and promote diversity by providing opportunities to underrepresented groups.

Cultural competence: The ability to understand, appreciate, and effectively work with people from diverse cultural backgrounds.

Inclusive language: Language that avoids stereotypes and promotes respect and inclusivity for all people, regardless of their gender, race, ethnicity, or other characteristics.

Intersectionality: The interconnected nature of social identities, such as race, gender, and sexual orientation, and how they overlap to create unique experiences of oppression and privilege.

Microaggressions: Small, often unintentional actions or comments that communicate negative attitudes or assumptions about a person's identity or background.

Tokenism: The practice of including a few individuals from underrepresented groups as a way of appearing diverse, without actually addressing systemic barriers to inclusion.

Unconscious bias: Implicit attitudes or stereotypes that affect our decisions and actions without our awareness or intention.

Workforce diversity: The variety of differences among employees in an organization, including differences in gender, race, ethnicity, age, ability, and other characteristics.

Workplace culture: The values, beliefs, behaviors, and practices that shape the social and psychological environment of a workplace.

Diversity equity and inclusion (DEI): The collective approach to promoting and ensuring a workplace that is diverse, equitable, and inclusive for all employees.

EEOC: Equal Employment Opportunity Commission, a federal agency that enforces laws against workplace discrimination.

Affirmative action: Policies and programs designed to increase the representation of historically disadvantaged groups in employment, education, and other areas.

Cultural competence: The ability to understand, appreciate, and effectively communicate with people from different cultures and backgrounds.

D&I metrics: Data and measurements used to track progress on diversity and inclusion initiatives, such as workforce demographics, employee engagement surveys, and retention rates.

Microaggressions: Subtle or indirect forms of discrimination, such as comments or behaviors that communicate bias or stereotype.

Supplier diversity: Programs and initiatives aimed at increasing the participation of minority-owned, women-owned, and other disadvantaged businesses in procurement opportunities.

Tokenism: The practice of hiring or promoting members of underrepresented groups primarily to create the appearance of diversity, rather than based on their qualifications or merit.

Unconscious bias: Implicit biases or attitudes that affect our perceptions and decision-making without our conscious awareness.

ABOUT THE AUTHOR

Felix Tih is an experienced communications and talent acquisition specialist with more than 12 years of work in different fields. He began his career as a journalist, where he honed his writing and storytelling skills.

After working as a journalist for a while, Felix switched to talent acquisition and quickly became known for his ability to find and hire top talent from a wide range of backgrounds. He has a proven track record of developing and implementing effective recruitment strategies that not only attract top talent but also foster a culture of inclusion.

In addition to his journalism and talent acquisition experience, Felix has also worked extensively as a mindset coach, helping individuals and teams achieve success by developing a growth mindset and overcoming limiting beliefs. Through his coaching, Felix has had the opportunity to work with a diverse range of people, from mid-career professionals to executives and entrepreneurs, helping them achieve their personal and professional goals.

In addition to his professional achievements, Felix is also a published author. His book, Personal Branding: Master Your Digital Presence, is a comprehensive guide to building and managing a personal brand in the digital age.

Felix has a vast educational background in Public Law, Human Resource Management, Project Management and Journalism.

Get in touch with Felix Tih on LinkedIn, Twitter, Instagram, or Book a Consultation Call felixtih.com

www.ingramcontent.com/pod-product-compliance
Lightning Source LLC
Chambersburg PA
CBHW071027220526
45467CB00004B/1550